While shepherds watched

Text: Nahum Tate? (1652–1715)

*Brass parts are available.

This music is copyright. Photocopying is illegal.

14

chim-ing Christ-mas bells; They cheer us on our heaven-ly way those chim - ing

sweet bells; They cheer us on our heaven-ly way those chim - ing

19 SOPRANO (v.6 only) Fine

bells. Ding dong ding dong ding dong ding-a dong-a ding-a dong-a ding!

S.A.T.B. UNIS.

bells, they cheer us on our heaven-ly way those chim - ing bells.

S. 24

A.

2. 'Fear not,' said he (for__
4. The heaven-ly babe you__

T.

B. Verse 2 only†

28

migh - ty__ dread had__ seized their trou - bled mind)__ 'Glad__
there shall__ find to__ hu - man view dis - played__ All__

*⌢ last time only
†Verse 4 is unaccompanied, *ad lib.*

This endris night

Sixteenth-century English carol
arr. Paul Trepte

*Brass parts are available.

why liest thou thus in hay?'
in

crib though I be laid.'

T. & B. UNIS. *mf*

3. The

f

Solo reed.

Coventry Carol

Sixteenth-century English carol
arr. Paul Trepte

*Brass parts are available.

D.C. al Fine

Carol for Emmaus

Words & melody: Selwyn Image (b. 1931)
arr. Paul Trepte

*Brass parts are available.

see the world's poor_ pressed tight in the sta - ble and_ crowd-ing the

door._ I see etched in_ their fa - ces_ the faith that I seek,_ with the trust of_ di -

-sci-ple-ship, the hope of the meek. Though the fox has his lair and the

birds have their nest, with the out-cast it is that Christ choos-es to rest.

nest, with the out-cast it is that Christ choos-es to rest.

Man.

Solo

Ped.

CHOIR I UNIS. *mf*

If I too would par-take of this gift and this pain, my

S.

A.

CHOIR II*

ah

T.

B.

sur-plus and life must help_ o-ther souls' gain, For by lov-ing and_ shar-ing with

(ah)_____ ah_____

* Choir II and/or organ/brass instruments

for the Ely Diocesan Choral Festival, 1993

My dancing day

English traditional carol
arr. Paul Trepte

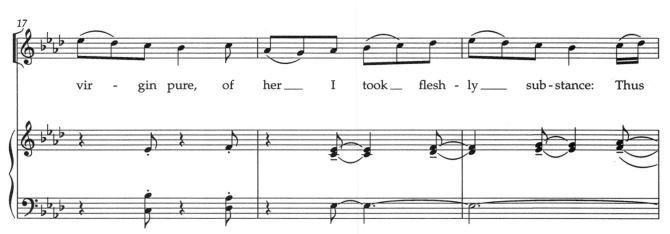

*or semi-chorus

was I knit to man's na-ture to call my true love to my dance: Sing

O my love, O my love, my love, my love, this have I done for my true love.

mf più legato

3.* In a man-ger laid and wrapped I was, so ve-ry poor this

ah

was my chance, Be-twixt an ox and a sil-ly poor ass to call my true love

ah

* Verse 3: organ doubles A.T.B. *or* perform unaccompanied.

to the dance: Sing O my love, O my love, my love, my love, this

ah

this

have I done for my true love.

ah

have I done for my true love.

ah

Man. *mf*

S.

A.

p

ah

T. & B.

UNIS.

mf

4. Then af - ter - wards bap - tized I was; the
(5.) thir - ty pence Ju - das me sold, his

p

Ped.

(Ped.)

Man.

5. For

6. *Be - fore Pi-late the Jews _ me brought, where Ba-rab-bas had _ de - li - ver-ance, They

scour-ged me and set me at nought, judged me to die _ to lead _ the dance: Sing

O my love, O _ my love, my love, my love, this have I done for my _ true love.

This have I done for my _ true love.

* Verse 6: organ doubles A.T.B. *or* perform unaccompanied.

Ped. (with 32')

* Organ doubles voices *ad lib.*

* Choir II is optional